...the city I'll never forget...

SAN FRANCISCO

The city and bay area
are renowned for their
stunning beauty, rising
from one of the most
beautiful natural harbors
in the world.

Rising from the enclave of one of the most beautiful natural harbors in the world, San Francisco epitomises the laid-back lifestyle of West Coast America. Sophisticated yet bohemian, progressive yet fiercely proud of its historical roots - the City, the Bay area and beyond, have become as renowned for their abundance of cultural and artistic pursuits, as for their stunning geographical beauty.

Constructed on the back of the 1850s gold rush, San Francisco's most lucrative and sustainable industry today is tourism. Each year over 16 million visitors flock to the city. The magnificent span of the Golden Gate Bridge, the elegant profile of the Coit Tower, and the distant silhouette of Alcatraz are all instantly recognisable as part of the San Francisco skyline. The cable cars that negotiate more than forty hills which comprise the city, trundle their way up and down precipitous streets to some of the most breathtaking views in the world.

A mecca for the arts, San Francisco's most notable achievements are in the area of literature and music. Psychedelic rock and roll, poetry, the Beat movement and the infamous "Summer of Love" remain enduring symbols of the foundations on which this cosmopolitan city are built. To this day popular culture in San Francisco revolves around music, the arts and food. The restaurants and bars of North Beach and Chinatown are as much a part of the experience of the City as the city itself.

In terms of geography and architecture, the city and surrounds easily live up to the reputation as one of Americas most spectacular regions. From the tranquil redwood groves of Muir Woods, the dramatic coastlines south to the Monterey peninsular, to the stark industrial skylines of Oakland and Alameda , the diversity of the area is a visitor's dream come true.

San Francisco has been shaped by its colorful history, and has an incomparable character not replicated anywhere in the world. This stunning collection of photographs by Peter Lik, captures the true spirit of the City through the eyes of one of the world's most accomplished landscape photographers.

SAN FRA

NCISCO

SAN FRANCISCO SUNRISE

The majestic Golden Gate Bridge sheds her blanket of fog and greets the morning, as a sudden burst of sun pierces the clouds.

GHIRARDELLI LIGHTS

Evening falls, and a thousand twinkling lights illuminate the Bay.

NORTH BEACH

A lasting reminder of San Francisco's colorful history.

OPPOSITE PAGE

HYDE STREET

As the island of Alcatraz dominates the background, a cable car negotiates the precipitous streets of the City.

PREVIOUS PAGE

BAY MORNING

The shimmering waters of San Francisco Bay, bask in
the tranquil reflections of sunrise. One of the most
beautiful natural harbors in the world, it is spanned at
its deepest point by the elegant contours of the famous
Golden Gate.

MOONLIT BRIDGE

The full moon casts a dramatic backdrop over the Bay.

ALAMO SQUARE

Restored to their former glory, a row of pastel hued Victorian houses on Hayes St is an elegant reminder of the City's past.

MORNING MIST

A lingering morning fog floats above the Bay,

shrouding the familiar arches of the Golden Gate.

PIGEON POINT LIGHTHOUSE

This guardian of the cliffs is framed by the yellow blooms that decorate the coastline south of San Francisco.

NAPA VALLEY

An idyllic morning in the picturesque

vineyards of the Napa Valley.

NAPA VINEYARD

As well as producing some of the finest wines in the world, Napa is renowned for its stunning scenery.

NAPA VALLEY BARN

An old water driven mill sits abandoned in

a secluded clearing.

MT TAMALPAIS

From the top of the mountain, sweeping views of the 6300-acre Mount Tamalpais State Park.

WINDMILLS

OPPOSITE PAGE

CITY LIGHTS

The lights of evening traffic illuminate the
sculptural arches of the Bay Bridge.

TRANSAMERICA PYRAMID

An iconic city landmark, The Pyramid climbs 853 feet into the air.

VISTA POINT

The majestic pylons of the bridge disappear into an enveloping fog.

BAY BRIDGE

The Bay Bridge connecting Oakland and San Francisco stretches for four and a half miles over the harbor.

RICHMOND BRIDGE

One of five crossings of the Bay, the elegant contour of the Richmond Bridge snakes its way across the harbor.

TRANQUIL HARBOUR

A lone yacht floats lazily off Sausalito Point, as the city skyscrapers catch the last rays of sun.

CALIFORNIA SEA LIONS

The famous California Sea Lions of Pier 39 bask in the sun and entertain the visitors.

HORSESHOE BAY

The early morning light gently brushes the coastline illuminating the shores of the Bay.

FISHERMANS WHARF

A hard working fishing fleet rests for the evening
beneath tranquil skies.

PIER 39

San Francisco's premier tourist attraction is home to the famous colony of California sea lions and the Peter Lik gallery.

FISHERMANS WHARF

The bustling marina of Fisherman's Wharf celebrates the city's maritime heritage.

OPPOSITE PAGE

MARINA REFLECTIONS

Fishing boats reflect their charm into the glassy waters of the Bay.

COIT TOWER

The famous memorial of Coit Tower sits atop Telegraph hill and commands

panoramic views of the Bay.

CABLE CARS

An enduring symbol of the city, the clanging bells of the cable cars herald their arrival as they trundle up and down city streets.

COASTAL SUNSET

A lone Cyprus tree stands silhouetted against the California sunset.

NEXT PAGE

PALACE OF FINE ARTS

The graceful architecture of the Palace of Fine Arts is one of the city's many cultural

attractions.

PREVIOUS PAGE

TWILIGHT ARCHES

Sunset provides a stunning painted backdrop for the delicate arches of the Golden Gate Bridge.

GLOWING TRACKS

The background hum of the cable car tracks is a unique aspect of the character of the city.

NEXT PAGE

LOMBARD STREET

Lombard Street twists and turns its way down the sharp incline, earning its reputation as the "crookedest street in the world."

SAUSALITO SUNSET

The gentle touch of sunset colors the view from Sausalito Harbour.

OPPOSITE PAGE

THE PYRAMID

The tallest building in the city, the Transamerica Pyramid soars into the evening sky.

THE BRIDGE

A close encounter with San Francisco's most
famous landmark.

THE BAY

A tranquil moment in the most beautiful harbor in the world.

SILENT NIGHT A row of antique lamps disappears into the shadows of the night.

SUNSET GLOW

The fiery San Francisco sun sinks beneath the golden arches of the bridge.

OPPOSITE PAGE

TREASURE ISLAND

From Treasure Island, the lights of the distant city illuminate the horizon.

CITY OF LIGHTS

As dusk falls, the jewel of the West Coast turns on her charm.

MT TAMALPAIS

The emerging peaks of the city skyline pierce the early morning fog in a stark contrast to the rolling hills of Mt Tamalpais State Park.

PREVIOUS PAGE

MUIR WOODS

The spectacular redwood groves of Muir Woods were declared a National Monument in 1908. The lungs of the
San Francisco area, they provide a soothing relief from the hustle and bustle of city life.

FOREST GIANTS

The massive Redwoods soar to
over 250 feet.

MT TAMALPAIS   A patchwork of over 200 miles of stunning walking tracks, Mt Tamalpais bathes in the aura of sunset.

CALIFORNIAN POPPY

Vibrant orange petals of a California poppy contrast

dramatically against an azure sky.

THE CONSERVATORY OF FLOWERS

The oldest building in Golden Gate Park, The Conservatory was originally

transported in crates from Ireland in 1876.

GOLDEN GATE BRIDGE

The remnants of an early morning fog cling to the arches of the Golden Gate Bridge as she stretches from Vista Point across to the City.

SAUSALITO

The Mediterranean style waterfront town of Sausalito offers magnificent uninterrupted views of Angel Island and San Francisco.

ALCATRAZ

Nicknamed "The Rock" the penal colony of Alcatraz boasts a colorful history. The "escape proof" prison ceased operation in 1963 and is now a major tourist attraction.

GOLDEN GATE REFLECTIONS

The striking reflections of the bridge color the
waters of Horseshoe Bay.

MOON OVER MT TAMALPAIS   A full moon hangs suspended high in the skies above Mt Tamalpais, bathing the landscape in an ethereal light.

BAKER BEACH

The incoming tide tumbles over rocks, creating a surreal foreground to this unusual view of the bridge.

ALAMO SUNSET

The restored Victorian houses of Alamo Square are an elegant reminder of days gone by. Many of these beautiful houses were lost in the earthquakes of 1906 and in the subsequent fires that ravaged the city.

INNER CITY   The old and the new stand side by side in a city renowned for its unique architecture.

PACIFIC COAST   The Pacific Ocean meets the West Coast in a moment of perfection preserved forever.

NEXT PAGE **LOST CITY**   From beneath a churning cauldron of cloud, the city rises to meet the day.

PETER LIK- BIOGRAPHY

Multi award winning Australian photographer Peter Lik, is internationally acclaimed for his distinctive and artistic landscapes. A self-taught master of photography, Lik is able to capture the true spirit of the land within the confines of his viewfinder. His work mesmerises and challenges the viewer in a way few other landscape photographers can.

Born in 1959 in Melbourne, Peter was given his first camera as a boy of eight and has barely put one down since. Throughout his life and through a variety of careers -including teaching and landscape gardening - Lik has retained a fascination and passion for photography. It was whilst travelling through Alaska in the early nineties, that he discovered a new and encompassing field of vision - the panoramic camera. In a chance meeting with a fellow photographer, he was entranced by the power of his panoramic images, and by that photographer's challenge - "Go big or go home". Lik chose to do both. He sold his van to buy the camera and returned to Australia determined to pursue a career in photography.

The birth of his own publishing company, established Lik as a leader in his field. It raised his profile to the extent that in 1999 he was able to fulfil a long held dream of opening his own Galleries. Now with Galleries worldwide his time is spent travelling, capturing the unique landscapes that have become his trademark.

Peter Lik's deep connection with the land is evident in his sensitive and compelling compositions. His respect for preserving the 'spirit of place' is a major defining factor in his work. Under Lik's practiced eye, every new day and every new location becomes a canvas in his never-ending search for the perfect image. Perhaps in his own words lies the secret behind this driven photographers success ....

"My search has just begun...."

Peter Lik Gallery

Peter Lik Galleries worldwide showcase the finest
work of this premier landscape photographer.

©PETER LIK PUBLISHING

PETER LIK IMAGES ARE EXCLUSIVELY REPRESENTED BY

 PETER**LIK**IMAGE**LIBRARY**

www.peterlikimages.com

DESIGN

       Shelley Jelonek, Artshak Design

       Email: info@artshak.com.au

       Website: www.artshak.com.au

TEXT

       Julietta Henderson

PHOTO EDITORS

       Cameron Le Bherz

       Julietta Henderson

       Steve (Merv) Moorhouse

ISBN 187658507-2

CALIF

ORNIA